A MAN THAT NEVER TAKES RISK IS A MAN WHO NEVER DOES ANYTHING AT ALL!

David Michael Pena

DEDICATION

To createspace.com for publishing and all the little people that made it happen

CONTENTS

ACKNOWLEDGMENTS

Thanks to createspace.com for publishing and me of course for editing, and all the people that made this possible. You know who you are!

INTRODUCTION

This book is on how the American government works and why the system is set up so the rich get richer and the poor get poor. The fact of the matter is that The American government needs the rich, so they're going to cater to them, give them tax breaks, why is that the lower your income is the higher percent tax you pay, well its simple only 3% of America makes over a 100,000 dollars a year so the need them to provide jobs for the middle class and poor. You see I'm not rich, yet, but I know I want to be rich because that's the only way to break out of the system of the Man keeping you down your whole live and then hopefully we can save up enough to retire and then have that fear that we're going to outlive our money. The only way is to get rich that's why I'm not where I wanna be yet, but we have to never stop hustling because that's where it's at, the top. You'll hear me say after a lot of my book I'll see you at the top and what that means is we have to get rich or bottom line the man will keep us down for ever. Now as I say they are the hustlers and the guaranteed paycheck workers, which work for a pay check. Now they can be wealthy but it's the self-employed are the ones who get rich and the people that own successful business. You see it's a common example of you want cake and eat it too, but the government is more concerned about the rich because if the take their businesses elsewhere then what happens to the middle class and poor, they will be yelling" we have no jobs" then there're going to be really screwed. The man is a group of aristocratic white males that's secretly run this country, now all of us heard of the secret societies like the free masons and others. This is all true they do exist and there all work together to keep the economy in motion. Now this is not a bad thing it's a good thing because if the government really let the people run the government we would be in big trouble. Many of you are saying American in trouble now we have a trillion dollar depict, and we know **Russia** and **China** have more money than us that's a perfect example of why **Obama** didn't push **Russia** out of Ukraine he's not going to bite the hand that feeds him and same with **China**. So this being said people come to America for one reason and that to take advantage of the free enterprise system which is the greatest in the world, and believe me I have learned that from living in monarchy which is still living the 1800's. If you say anything about the king or royal family you can be imprisoned. I know an American living here in Thai land said something negative about the king son and he's still in prison. I'm still living in Thailand but the royal family has a lot of dirt that I can tell you about and I just would like to say for the record "I love the king and would never say anything negative about him or his family. That's my disclaimer you don't want to see a brother get locked up do ya?

But if you live in America,
Don't take what you have for
granted.

This chapter is called hood rich vs. real rich, now what hood rich is, is someone that makes good money but they spend it as fast as they get it. When I was about 22 years old my friend bought a new Camero at the time 2001. Now 15 years ago he had a 600 dollar car payment and one day he asked me for gas money, and I thought to myself, this mother fucker is driving a $20,000 car and he can afford to put gas in. And I love the guy I saw at the gas station and he had Benz clk and he put 8 dollars in the tank. But that's a person that will never obtain real riches because he spending everything he got to look cool in front of everyone else. We I learned a long time ago that I can't go around trying to impress everyone because at the end of the day the only person you need to impress is yourself, Why they're put 8 dollars in the tank, and I'm filling up my 1987 pick-up, I know I got 10,000 dollars in my savings account and I don't need anyone to know that. Why do we give a shit on what other people think, and if were trying to be fancy to attract a mate, is that the mate you really want, one that see's what you have and not you as a person. I've been there before and even if the sex is amazing you truly never are happy. Hood rich is the guy that cashed his 1000 check and put a new stereo in that bumps and cost 899 dollars, a and he right back where he stared, broke, and I did this for my years although I don't regret anything I have done in my life if I had made some minor changes I could be a millionaire already, but we can't cry over spilled milk the thing we need to do is change it, now I 'have been in the world of selling my whole life, I was the guy who if I saw something I could get low wholesale and a good mark up on it excited me. Making money excites me anyway when I became an author and my 1st book sold I was so excited not because I made a couple bucks but I started adding up I sell 10,000 copies and make x amount and if I ever sold a million I could make this amount, and so on and I don't care what anyone says money buys a lot of happiness, but I always say money can buy happy, but it can't but true love and I think without true love we are never truly happy. So what can we do to have real riches, the first is buy real-estate as soon as you can afford too, and that's income and tax breaks right there. Another thing that thing if you self-employed of course you can clam what you want, but if you 1099 the "man knows exactly how much you made, so to cut down on the taxes get a business name, now everything you buy including there is a section you can even write off travel , meals, and entertainment. The 'is no way for the "man" to know if it was business or not as long as you have a receipt you're in the clear. Now this brings us to be next chapter the IRS.

The IRS is the most ruthless government agency there is. You must pay your taxes, and believe me I had a run in with the IRS. I have always seen stories of red Foxx and will smith where they didn't pay their taxes and the literally they will come in your house and take everything you own and then freeze you bank account so you can't get any money, this is what happen to me I had 2,900 dollars in my checking account and I go to the bank and the ATM won't give me any money so I'm pissed of I go marching into the bank and the lady informs me that the IRS has frozen my bank account. You see I worked for a 1099 but never really made much so I just never filed and nothing ever happened, big mistake because I had a good year and I made 39,444 on my 1099 and once they see you making some money they want their cut and lets just say about

3 months later of being issued that 1099 with 39,444 on it, and BAAM the bank account frozen and the bank can't help you and then I; realized the "man "owns the banks so they can do whatever they want. This next part goes out to the people that make their money illegally, now I have made money illegally and legally, but now for the record it is all legal for me. Now if you have a job and make money on the side it's probably won't draw a red flag, but if you don't have a 9-5 or a 1099 you have to throw some of the money in the bank and pay taxes on it, now that being said

the "man doesn't give a shit on how you make you money he just wants his 20% and as long as the get that they stay off your back and you'll be fine. A classic example is Al Capone, this is man who killed hundreds of people and sold drugs, organized crime you name it, and there wasn't a problem until they found out he made 10 million dollars last year and didn't pay tax on it and then we have a problem, The "man" doesn't get his money then all hell is going to break loose, so they finally locked him up for tax evasion. They didn't give a shit that the money came from cocaine, they're just pist they didn't get the 20%. So it's a lesson learned but get the business name that's how the rich get richer, you'll notice people these days will have an s-corps, c-corps 5 LLC's. Why do they do this? The more business the more tax breaks that's why? Another good one that people are doing is; you notice now it's the Rev. Steve Harvey and it's the Rev. Al Green. Now they claim it because they want to "serve the lord". That's a crock of bullshit they do it now this separates then from church and state now they are tax exempt a huge tax break now when the want a kick back of payed for some it's you don't have to pay me just donate to my church and **BOOM** tax fee, beautiful way to beat the "MAN". Now most politicians and government officials have charities and phony foundations, its away to take free money you can't bribe a politician but you can make big contribution to their charity. Wink wink.. So they rich know how to take advantage of the system so I'm sorry to tell you but the middle class and poor will always pay a higher percent tax that's how American was set up and it has to be that way or the system will break down. Don't be surprised if you pick one of my books in the future and I'm the Rev. Dave Pena, I serve the lord and you must pull out you wallets and give give giiivvee. I kid, but it's a smart thing to do because now the government can't touch any of the "churches" assets. Now Hope fully you know that the American government is a democracy created for the people and ran by the people, lol, I can't even say it with a straight face it's such a crock of bullshit. Even the congress controls the presidential election the people waste the time vote and think there are making a difference, but in relatedly if the people really controlled the government we'd be in real trouble, because everyone in the country wants to be rich but no one wants to work for it so it you want to pay less taxes you got to make more money that's the bottom line, every presidents says change change and they don't change shit because that's the way the system was put together 300 years ago and will continue to be that way for the next 300 now there's little thing we do as people and in our community's to help, I not saying everything is useless so just give up and do nothing. I simply saying stop whining about being poor, the only way to beat the American system is get rich, I sell books t-shirts anything I can get my hands on where I can make a profit, I'm climbing my way to the top my way to the top, and that's what we need to do. Now this book is called A man that never task risk is a man that never does anything, if you a person that has a 9-5, that's ok but just remember that's all you ever have, you might have a good life, but you never be real rich, and I going to talk about real rich vs. hood rich again for a moment real rich is investment I had a lot of failures and successes in my life but one of my claim to fame that I'm proud of is my investment in Facebook and how I got out just in time, it took me about 2 years but a 300% return from Facebook stock and I made about 12,000 dollars off a 3,500 investment and that's when I realized I like letting my money work for me now yes you can lose money in the stock market and I knew almost for a fact that I would not see the day where Facebook was going out of business, so put your money somewhere where it's not liquid you can't spend or with draw it from an ATM because that's where we get ourselves in trouble. Now this last section I call the mad rapper, this is a guy always complain why he didn't get a loan why did so and so get because I'm black. Now we have to stop playing the race care I have a that every ting happen because he's Mexican, oh he didn't get job because he's Mexican, and he go pulled over by the cops because he's Mexican, which can be true in some instances , but I'm a triple minority so can

I can pull that shit all day long, but it doesn't get us anywhere, the bottom line is simple when you go to the bank to borrow money, the first thing they're going to do is pull your credit and see if you pay people back, see a credit report is important, they wanna see if you have a history of paying people back or you have a history of not people back, it's that simple. If a person ask to borrow 20 dollars and you know he owes 5 other people 20 dollars and hasn't played them back in 6 months, you don't wanna lend them the money that's plain and simple and they look at how much money you make and how many payments you have and are you making them on time, they're no fools if they are lending you the money they want it back they're not like you buddies that will just forget about it later, they make their money on the interest of the loan. I never seen a black person that has good credit pays his bill on time and makes decent money not get approved, it the black guy that tries to live above his means and has a Benz he's 3 month's late on the payment and can't pay his sears card on time because he always charging it up, and the when he doesn't get approved he takes off yeah I didn't get the loan because I was black. No you did't, get it because you don't pay for shit and you can even keep up on the Benz payment you have now where does that leave you to pay the bank back. Now white people understand this now I'm not saying black have bad credit but they have more of history being hood rich, because you see the video's and that's what these guys want well all that shit in the video's is rent including the Jewelry, I even seen a guy packing up the gold chains after the video shoot and taking off with it, you got to understand there is no way these guys made enough before the record even comes out to buy a mansion and a lambo, and Rolls Royce there is no way is a Fas ad, all the shit is rented so don't spend all you money trying to be like them because that shit the don't even own yet and can afford to own yet. So if you have an 87 pick-ups and studio apartment, it doesn't matter keep 10 G's in the bank and let these guys try to be fancy and show of because there always be one paycheck away from being broke.

I want to share one more thing that you'll hear me mention a lot is **PMA** and that stands for positive mental attitude and that is a necessity in life. You can be one who waits for thing to happen or a person that makes things a happen, you see you attitude will determine you altitude. It's not what happens to you in life its how you deal with it. I have had a very interesting life and you can read all about in my autobiography. How did I become a drug selling pimp? Don't let the title fool you but there is more to it than that but one thing after spending my time in prison and the police taking everything I had, I had to start from scratch and the first success I had was a book tell about my travels and how I ended up in southeast Asia working in a life of drugs and prostitution one thing I relisezed some time we don't appreciate what we have and we're always bitching about the things we don't have. But a wise man once told me he said " Dave is you wanna have all the good things in life you have to start appreciating the things you already have or you'll never have anything" and now I know what he meant, you see we make a lot of mistakes in our life because we don't listen to people and we think there just saying that to make money of us and in turn it may be true, but no matter what you do in life someone's always going to make money of you so the best thing to do is worry about how much you're making and how you can sell more instead what everyone else is making that's a mistake I made early on in my career when I went to prison unfortunately it's not America where you have rights or you innocent until proven guilty, you don't get a trial or a lawyer there go by the evidence the police has and he makes the judgment without ever going in front of a judge, and the can take everything legally and even go to the bank and with draw all you money. Now some of us that are reading this book are having success and are reading for more positive information and if that's the case you are going places and never stop learning and you're on the way to the top. That said there is the person that is reading this now that is not having success, and is late on his car payment, wife wants him to quit and get a "Real Job", and for that person this is more important for you, because I been there. I have had times of success and positivity and nothing could bring me down, and I have lost everything and had failures and had my bank account go from 6 digits to 3 digits. They only one thing that was the difference when I had 6 figures in the bank and 3 digits was my attitude PMA controls everything you say and everything you do. This stands for positive mental attitude. There is nobody in this world that is successful, and hasn't had failures. It's something we all must go through to have success, the trick is having more successes than failures, for some of us it will happen in our younger years and some mid-age and some at 55, no matter how long it takes you to become successful, just don't stop trying. There's no problem with failing, but there is problem for people who don't dust themselves off and try again. Now I'm not going to spew about how much money I have and bullshit people into believing if you buy this book you instantly become rich. I'm just going to share with you the things I learned from other people and some I have come up with myself that have worked for me over the years.

I have done many things in my life to make money some legal and some illegal. There is nothing wrong will wanting wealth, and I don't care what anyone says I said it before money can buy happiness and I have bought a lot of happiness in my life. There is only one thing money can't buy and that's TRUE LOVE. But I won't touch that one for now I'll save that for my next book. Now since I have be young I've always been fascinates in buy and selling things I could get a good low wholesale price and could have a good mark up on. It starts in school there's always the candy man. The boy that realizes I can buy the bag of lollipops and it only cost me 8 cents and I can sell them in the school yard for a quarter. These are the future business owners, not that they will always become rich but there people that know how to make money and ones that provide for their Families. Now if this was you, you know what I'm talking about. Now there are two types of people that work for someone and people that work for them self and there is one more I forgot and that's the mixture of the two which is very common. This is a man or woman who has a rag 9-5 and has his own business on nights a weekend, like my uncle Jim, who drove a UPS truck by day and on the weekends was DJ Jamming Jimmy. I'm not going to tell you this ways is right or this way is wrong, but the fact is I haven't met too many rich employees. Now when sold weed housed black jack tables in my apartment, work for companies and sometimes had 2 or 3 things going at a time my motto id I have nothing better to do than make money so if I could buy something low and sell high I was game. Now I had done all sorts of things but when I turned 20 I would start working for working for a legitimate business and learning not just how to make money but the most important thing I learned was how to teach other people to make money. There was a supervisor that worked for the company and would smoke big cigars and wear all these crazy suits, but I knew one thing I want to have a Cadillac like the one he was driving and I' don't care what anybody says but nothing rides smother than a Cadillac, American engineering at its finest. He told me "Dave, you can have anything life you want if you help enough people get what they want".

This book is a lot to handle, which means some people aren't going to like it because like the old saying goes the truth hurts. Everyone always will have failures, and that's ok but not ok to lie down and give up. Now most of our parent's is like the poor dad, get an honest day pay for an honest day's work. This is where the title of the book comes in.

Now people that work by the hour or for a salary are not risk takers, they want the guaranteed pay check every week. This doesn't mean they stupid or bad people but that's what separates the poor-middle class from the rich. Most of this book is about risk taking but it's about just plain old stacking chips and how to make so money. Now the I worked for was Mr. Lipinski and I owe him for most of the information I'm about to share , with a Dave Pena spin on it America is the greatest country in the world and living in another country for a brief time,

I'll tell you now don't take it for granted. Now if you're in America you have the right to free speech and free press, Thank god for the internet I can still take advantage of the American free enterprise system. So the next time you don't wanna make that last sales call, or knock on that door, or go show a house on a Sunday, you better thank you lucky stars that you live in country of free enterprise and that you can even have the opportunity to knock a door. That said, now when I started my boss' name was Mr. Lipinski he wasn't a millionaire, but in the 11 years I worked for him I watched him go from driving a powder blue 1973 Chevy van, to a porches Carrera, the $120,000 edition those that now cars know they refer to it as the J-lo edition. Now when I was new my first month was a little shaky with my commission earnings and this is a great example of risk taking. I made a little money and I was new and not used to working on commission so it not that I didn't money it's just that I spent it and partied most of my money away. So of course when I need the money I have a slow week, so now I'm in a bind, I thought maybe I would ask him for the money because at this point I was outta options so I go knock on the door to his office and he says come in, I go in and I reply to him "do you have a minute". I explained that I have to give my roommate at the time 600 dollars to cover my share of the rent. He doesn't say yes or no and just stairs at me for what seemed to be the longest 30 seconds of my life then he grabs his check book, still hasn't said a word yet. At this point I think either he is paying his light bill or he's going to give me the money, I wasn't sure yet, then he hands it to me I looked at it and it was made for $1000 dollars then says, "I like what you're doing and right now I'm still growing but I see you as one of my future managers, buy some shirts and ties with the rest. You see I could have cashed that check and be outta there but he took that risk. Now if he told me no he might have lost a great dealer/ manager. Did he make money off me of course, but it started with the risk he took on me, some risk you take don't work out but when you take risks great things can happen, Coronal Sanders was trying to start his first **KFC** and everyone to him how he can't do it and why it won't work, he finally found an investor that took the risk of putting up the money, and for that man we all now **KFC** is one of the biggest most powerful fast food chains in the world, what if that investor never took that risk. Now like I said most of our families want to protect us, it's not that they don't want you to succeed, it's just they don't want to see you fail. Now I'm taking a risk with this book and the publishing company is taking a risk because they have to make 20 copies and if no one buys on copy they stuck with a stack of paper. But if you reading this I sold at least one copy. Now when I was new in the selling world my mom had girlfriend who one time brought her punkass boyfriend to one of my dad's famous cook outs. Now he's not rich but he makes a 100,000 a year and he tries to talk to me, and I tell him what I do and he says you do all the work and your boss makes all the money. At this time everything he says is blah, I wanna plug my ears and start singing the Sam Smith song la lalalalla. Now news flash if you don't want some to make money off you then is your own boss, and even then the company you buy your inventory from is making money off you. Don't focus on what other people are making focus on what you're making. Now my boss had season tickets to the dodgers and would invite me sometimes. Now the idea of being you own boss is so that you can do whatever you like and go home and knowing as you're watching T V money is being made, it's a great feeling you seem to have better rest. I was a manager for him and its great feeling to know you making money even when you not working, I recall one time at a dodger game I got a sales call from a dealer and we got the contract. Of course I was happy now that I was the manger I made a commission on everything sold in the company, so I ran back to seat to tell him, he said did you get the contract. I reply yes, and then we smile and smack are beers together, and he says "welcome to good life Pena", it's at that point I realized money makes me happy and I like it made for me around the clock.

When I started I took a risk I company where if I didn't sell I didn't make money. He's another news flasher if you work for a salary and you company doesn't sell any product you too won't make any money, because you be out of a job. Now yeah I worked at a burger joint but still 80% of the people told me to say with the guaranteed $250 a week at the burger joint. Now I won many contest and traveled all over the United States, New York Chicago, New Orleans, Las Vegas, Palm Springs, Lake Tahoe, and Hawaii three times all expenses paid. Now if I listen to everyone and didn't take that risk would the jack in the box company have sent me all over the country, probably not? Now the money I won't talk about but I lived wild and crazy and if take the coke that went up my nose and the booze I put away in 10 years that's a million I lost for sure. But I had fun and met most of the best people in my life there and wouldn't trade it for the world I have no regrets. The last couple of years have been a learning experience, and then something happen to me, that would change my life. It all starts about 6months ago I owned a bar so now I took my favorite thing to do and made it my job I would get dunk and entertain everyone. You know the old saying if you love what you do it's not work. Well I start experiencing stomach pains bad and thru the months and it gets worse and worse, until one day it's so bad that I think that I'm going to pass out. So I go to the hospital tell the doctor I'm having stomach pains and he starts like feeling my stomach and he ask me what do I eat normally and do I drink alcohol, and if I smoke. I say you mean cigarettes, and he says" yes". For some reason Thai's don't get my sarcastic humor. Then he x-ray's me and then leaves for about 10 min and comes back with X ray in his hand and says you see that. "You know what that is" I said "it looks like a black ball or something I don't know"; he says "you have a stomach ulcer". He asked how much do you drink? I'm think to myself this is going to sound like a jerk boys skit, I say well I drink beer during the day and put a big dent in a tequila bottle at night. He's says every day, Yes" I mumbled. So he says you can live with an ulcer or you can have it surgical removed but if you decide to live with it, the drinking has to stop or its going to tear up your stomach lining. I thought yeah yeah fuckin doctor's always tell you don't smoke and drink same old shit so I tested it I stop drinking for two days then started again and sure enough right after about one or two beers the pain would come back. So the life that I had been had taken a toll on my body so I had to give up the best job I ever had, "drinking".

Well I believe in two things karma and everything happens

for a reason, but it's not what happens to in life, buts its how you deal with. This book is about stuff you already knew and sometimes we just need to be reminded or hear someone else say it. My boss used to higher motivational speakers and then after they were done people would say how amazing there are and they're going to do everything he said. Then after the meeting he would tell me I say the same thing he says every day and he comes up and says its and its gold to everyone. But most of us want to listen to rich people, and don't get wrong it's a good thing to listen to successful people, but I learned one rule of business from a man who wasn't rich, it was if you cannot mark up 3 times you can't afford to stay in business and its true, what this means is if you have an overhead and a payroll, let's say whole sale you product cost 100 you cannot take less that 300 dollars for it and if whole sale is 350 you can't take less than 1050 for and so if you do you will find yourself out of business. Now if you a retail sore you just put the price at 1050 and that's that, but if your selling real estate or a direct sales in home you have to leave little room for price because if you selling people don't tell you no because they don't want it, they tell you no to see what you'll do next. Now I sold a high ticket items so we had payment plans for people that couldn't afford to pay cash. I can't tell you how many people told me they couldn't afford 100 dollars a month then after all my discounts they say ok, but I'll just write a check for all of it. They couldn't afford 100 dollars but now she can write me a check for $1500. But she doesn't want to tell me I really want it bad and if give me a discount I'll probably will buy it. Whether you're sell real estate to a customer or take a customer for a test drive or in a home, direct selling, as long as there is a prospect in front of you its guaranteed a sale is going to be made you either make a sale to the customer or the customer sells you on why they can't purchase today. That's why you should always be studying and learning because often times the customer is the better sales person. Now one thing when I was new in selling that helped me win customers and helped in managing people. It was taught me by a man named Patrick white; it's called the power of touch. And you can test but I'll tell you something about touching someone that you can get them to turn into putty in your hands, I have had it done to me and it works every time. Now this is not a sexually thing in anyway. It's kind of a light touch I recommend it on the knee or shoulder but you make anyone answer a question exactly the way you want. I'll give you an example, this minivan has four air bags and tested for safety because no matter what the cost is we can't put a price on our family's heath can we? Now right before the can we is the light touch on the shoulder and people will give the answer you want every time. I'll share a story I was in a home giving a presentation a big 300 pound Samoa man just sat the arms fold the whole time and then I asked him to give it a try and I put my hand out like I was going to shake his hand and I pulled him up out of the chair and I got the first smile out of him. Not that I didn't listen, but we forget some of the things we already know sometimes we just need to be reminded of them so I kept asking questions and doing the slight taps on the shoulder and I'll tell you what it hasn't stirred me wrong now it's a light tap on the shoulder or knee area, don't go grabbing vagina's and penis's say that's what the sales book told me to do. Now if you showing a product to a customer, and they don't buy, then they go to another dealer ship and buy the same car, or you do a in home presentation and they don't buy from you but they buy from the next person who comes knocking at their door. It's the same car; it's the same cleaning system. The only thing that's different is the standing in front of the product. I don't can how good the product is your selling nothing sells itself. People wanna do business with successful people and no one does business with people they don't like. Never tell people you're selling to make cash. But it's ok to tell a customer you goals. Most real estate and direct sales company have sales contest. If you work for a company that doesn't have contest I would probably choose something else I would consider it a must and its some many thing's because now you don't want take the order with them so I can make quick cash, it a now factor, they reason is my office is having a contest takes the most orders or if I take 24 orders this month they giving away a free trip to Disney land and boy I would really like to take my son. I can't tell you how many times after I would take any order they would say I hope you win the bike or hope you win the trip to Disney land send me a post card people love successful people and winners, I know I do. Don't get me wrong no one is going to buy from you just because if they do you will win bike, it's a reason to sigh a contact to day and not next month and most of all there nothing like getting reward for the hard work, If you in Hawaii on the beach drinking a pina cola while

Start the dam think we get ever drove everyone else it stuck back working it's a priceless feeling. If you are the owner of a direct sales company and don't have contest get one immediately, and it you're company has them already you're in the right spot, push everything will fall in to place when you win contest you family will love you. He's phrase you never hear you taking me on too many vacations and you making too much money you need to quit.

The man I worked for I worked for didn't become rich overnight. People want to get rich now, but there are no get rich quick scams and believe me I've tried them all. I call it instant gratification. I don't know at what point he became a million and he never officially announced it, but after he bought a m6 Bow and a 850, 000 condo the next day I realize that's probable not the last million he had. In ten years he owned sport's cars big that you would almost need a ladder to get into but I'll share a funny story with you he calls the office and says to I go a new ride so said what you get this time he says you see and pulls up in a 2009 Chevy corvette and mean new because it was at the time 2008. Now he always would say he take it for a spin and throw me the keys and I think it was a motivational tool he used but hot dam it pumped me up every time, but this time he didn't throw me the keys and said you going to let me take it for a spin and I could tell he didn't want too he says ok but I'm going with you we jump in and I have drove fast cars but till this Day it's the fastest car I have drove. So as soon as I figure out of how to start the fucken thing, we take off out of the parking lot and I decide let's see what this thing can do and I floor it at a stop sign and my head literally go sucked in to the seat and that thing took off like a jet I almost could slow down at the next stop sigh. And then came to a complete stop and he looked over at me like he was going to take his knife out and stab me and calm says "please don't do that again" and the test drive came to an end a little quick, BUT all I could talk about was how fast **MIKE'S NEW** corvette was for the next two weeks. Now I share these stories with you because all the successful people I knew had to take a risk at one point to get where there were. IT'S like a customer telling you they can't buy because what if the loose there job and can't pay for it. They took the risk when they bought the house, because he could get injured on the job and he can pay the mortgage and loos the **HOUSE**, or fall behind in property tax and the government takes it. They took that risk when the bought that minivan in the driveway, But a man person that doesn't take risk, never does anything, they just let life go by although I have had many failures but I'll never stop taking risk. The last thing I'm going to give you some of classic quotes that hopefully will help you and the defiantly helped me the fit on is today is the tomorrow you were talking ABOUT YESTERDAY. How many times have we stopped making a sales call or stopped knock on a door and said let's call it a night and we'll make happen tomorrow. What this quote means is you every day we keep saying were going to push hard to morrow but that tomorrow never come you have push every day like it's the 30 the of the month tomorrow is not an option. IT'S like the sigh I used to have that used to say free beer tomorrow so if some asked I say OH THAT'S tomorrow but as we all know that tomorrow never comes. Another one is "YOU can make money or excuses but you can't make both" WHAT this means if other people are having success, and I'm not we don't take responsibility so we blame everyone else and I've done this be for. It's because my boss is a jerk, this is a shitty area we are working, so and so gets all the good leads and the give the crappy ones. If you not having success but other people in your company are I'm sorry to say but it's you, it's not your boss, it's not the pay program, it's not area the problem is you making bullshit excuse instead of getting off your ass and making it happen. You can never achieve any kind of a goal until you can take responsibility for you action. If you don't win you contest don't start making excuses say to yourself this month I got to make that extra push and maybe work some Sundays. Because when you start making excuses IT'S hard to make money. When you stop making excuse and are responsible for your own action that's when you can improve yourself. The third one is" you can either sore with the eagles or flop with the turkey". Now this one I didn't get right away and after about year I started to learn what this meant. IT'S about hanging around with negative people vs. positive people. Every company has the complains corner I call it that the one the bitch about how they can't pay there, they had that sales yesterday but the manager came in and ruined it all, and so and so if fucking the boss so there getting all the good leads all those people are do is flop and flop because they have negative attitudes and the other group is the ones where the dealer is showing every the watch he just one in a contest or outside showing everyone the new truck the bought, you never catch An eagle in the back bitching about their paycheck or how they knocked on a door and this lady yelled at them. So if you catch yourself doing it stop it eagles soar to great heights and turkeys flop and never move up off the ground, which one do you wanna be? Now the 4th one IS: the hard you work the luckier you get". What this means is if you're in the world of selling there is no such thing is luck. You get luck by working had. Have you ever seen a sales person that's goes out every day and knocks on the very first door and get the sale 7 days a week, or a sales person that makes a sale on the very first phone call every single day, nope I didn't thinks so. If that were the case that's luck, but we all **KNOW THERE** is no such thing as luck in the sales world. If you're in real estate and **YOU KNOCK** on a for sale by owner's house and get the listing it was because you out talking to people and not in the office on your easy chair waiting for the phone to ring like all the other agents, you were on the grind knocking on doors and talking to people working hard that's why you got lucky. This is perfect example of An eagle, then when you run back to the office pumped up and positive and tell everyone you got a new listing, the turkey's will be there with their negativity and have something to say, " it's a dump she never sell it or she'll have to take a low offer she'll never make any money and try to kill you positivity, and the truth is deep inside they know that they're being lazy just sitting in the office and you are making money, so the try to justify it. But don't listen to they're flopping, just walk away and use one of my favorite quotes I use to say when the guys would do that, is, "don't player hate congratulate, and then walk away. Then it leave no to keep going on with the others guys when you leave. And number five is the title of the book, a person who doesn't take risk is a person who never does anything at all , now this book is all about what that means. I' can tell numerous times I want to call it a day and knock the last door at 8:30 PM and made a sale, was I luck no I was working that sale never would have taken place if I fold it up and said will get tomorrow, as we all know you have to treat today lie it was today you were talking about yesterday, I have never met A person that has achieved great thing's. And hasn't taken risks. That's why if you reading this book I'm just the same as you. I'm using what I learned so far to become success full I'm on the climb with up alongside of you. Most books that you read are the finished product, the people are already rich. Then there are the scams buy my book and you become instantly rich like me, I'm not bullshitting anyone or claiming to have a yacht and a Rolls Royce. I have a saying "I'm not yet where I wanna be, BUT thank god I'm not where I used to BE. So grab my hand and I'll grab your hand and let's throw away all the excuses AWAY AND bust our asses, GET out make some sales, HAVE some fun and I'll see you at top!